WOODS, SHORE, DESERT

A Notebook, May 1968

Thomas Merton
with photographs by the author

Foreword by Brother Patrick Hart
Introduction and Notes by Joel Weishaus

MUSEUM OF NEW MEXICO PRESS
SANTA FE

Materials by Thomas Merton copyright © 1982 by the Trustees of
the Merton Legacy Trust. Other materials copyright ©
1982 Museum of New Mexico Press.

Printed in the United States of America.

Library of Congress Cataloging in Publication Data

Merton, Thomas, 1915-1968.
    Woods, Shore, Desert.

    Includes bibliographical references.
    1. Merton, Thomas, 1915-1968. 2. Monks—United
States—Biography. I. Title.
BX4705.M542A35   1982   271'.125'024 [B]   82-14200
ISBN 0-89013-140-6
ISBN 0-89013-139-2 (pbk.)

Museum of New Mexico Press
P.O. Box 2087
Santa Fe, New Mexico 87503

CONTENTS

FOREWORD

The typescript of this journal of two weeks written in May of 1968, less than six months before his Asian journey, was the last journal writing that Thomas Merton corrected and approved for publication. Father Merton dictated these passages, which had been selected from a larger journal, onto a dictaphone and they were then transcribed by his secretary. The journal entries were made at the Redwoods Abbey, a Cistercian convent in northern California, and later while visiting a small isolated Benedictine monastery, Christ in the Desert, at Abiquiu, New Mexico. While at the latter, Merton had an opportunity to meet Georgia O'Keeffe in her adobe home and studio not far from the monastery, and actually photographed her . . . out of focus! Fortunately he was more successful in his other attempts, as the photography in this volume bears witness.

The concluding entries in this journal may leave the reader somewhat mystified since Merton raises questions, something quite characteristic of him, without attempting to answer them directly; he believed that we are better known by the questions we ask than by the ready answers we often give. When preparing this manuscript for publication, it was consequently decided to situate Merton's trip to California and New Mexico in May of 1968 within the broader context of his monastic and solitary life at Gethsemani, and thus provide the reader with the background necessary for a better understanding of his journalistic comments.

In January 1968, Abbot James Fox resigned his post as Abbot of Gethsemani, and the community elected Flavian Burns as his successor. The new Abbot believed that Merton himself should be more actively involved in the decision making in regard to accepting or rejecting invitations to speak outside the monastery, or to visit and give retreats to other monastic communities in the future. At the same time, shortly after the abbatial election, Merton began discussing with the new Abbot the possibilities of a more isolated hermitage in view of the fact that the present one was too accessible to retreatants, old friends and casual visitors. Under the new legislation, it was now possible to live in a hermitage at some distance from one's monastery, even in a foreign country, as two monks of Gethsemani have subsequently done, one in Mexico and another in Papua New Guinea.

With the Abbot's approval, then, Merton planned a trip to California and New Mexico, in part to explore the possibilities these places might offer for a more remote solitude. Keeping this situation in mind, the journal entries in this volume take on a deeper meaning, especially when he writes in his concluding paragraph: "But I do have a past to break with, an accumulation of inertia, waste, wrong, foolishness, rot, junk, a great need of clarification of mindfulness, or rather of no mind—a return to genuine practice, right effort, need to push on to the great doubt. Need for the Spirit. Hang on to the clear light!"

It is a commonplace in monastic literature that the early Egyptian desert dwellers, soon after finding a place of solitude, were sought out by disciples, and before long these spiritual fathers (and mothers) were surrounded by groups of disciples seeking "a word of salvation." This would often dismay the masters, who in turn would then abandon their hermitages in search of even more remote places in the desert. Although Thomas Merton's case is not an exact parallel, there is some truth in the fact that once his reputation spread abroad and his hermitage was easily discovered by both seekers of true wisdom and the simply curious, he began to desire greater solitude. Merton's continuing search for God in solitude can be more easily understood if considered within this monastic tradition.

Brother Patrick Hart
Abbey of Gethsemani

INTRODUCTION

During May of 1968 Thomas Merton took a trip to California and New Mexico, his first extended, unattended time away from the Abbey of Gethsemani in twenty-six years. Later the same year he was to make a longer sojourn, one that would take him to Asia, where, in Bangkok, Thailand, on December 10, 1968, he would touch a faulty electric fan in his room and pass from this world.

So many biographies and critiques of Thomas Merton's life and work have been written that I feel it redundant to go into any details exclusive of the period covered by the book at hand. But a very brief summary of his life before May 1968 may be helpful.

Thomas Merton was born in Prades, France, on January 31, 1915. His father was an artist from New Zealand; his mother, also an artist, an American. She died when Tom was six, after which the boy traveled with his father or was shuttled between relatives. When he was sixteen his father died, leaving supervision of Tom to his godfather. Merton finished public school in England, then, after a summer in Italy, entered Clare College, Cambridge. But his godfather "decided that the temptations of Cambridge undergraduate life were too compelling."[1] In December 1934 Merton arrived in New York to live with relatives on Long Island while attending Columbia University. He received his B.A. in 1938, and an M.A. in English literature the following year.

On December 10, 1941, the young fun-loving man who seemed destined for a successful academic career took a train to Kentucky, where he disappeared behind the walls of the medieval Trappist monastery, the Abbey of Our Lady of Gethsemani. Behind those walls, during the next twenty-seven years, Thomas Merton, living under a strict rule of silence, wrote more than fifty books: essays, journals, biographies, poetry. His views as a civil rights and anti-war advocate became known throughout the world. And, along with his concerns with secular issues, Merton was perhaps the most important Christian mystic of our time.

In the early 1960s, while keeping up his prodigious writing and reading and his normal duties as priest and monk, Merton took on the demanding job of Master of Novices. All this combined to threaten seriously his rather fragile health, as well as his spiritual progress. In 1960 he was granted permission to spend some time in seclusion in a small cinder-block house on the monastery's grounds. By August 1965, finally relieved of his teaching responsibilities, he was able to spend most of his time living the eremitic life. But the popularity of his books was bringing more and more pilgrims to the gates of Gethsemani to see the famous monk. On May 6, 1968, "seeking a more solitary place for his hermitage, with the approval of his Abbot,"[2] Merton began a fifteen-day trip to the California coast and New Mexico desert.

In 1978 I came upon an article in *New Mexico Magazine* entitled "Thomas Merton's New Mexico."[3] Along with the text were a few photographs Merton had taken while visiting there. Upon my inquiring, the Thomas Merton Studies Center in Louisville, Kentucky, informed me that a series of photographs Merton had taken in California and New Mexico, along with a notebook, were possibly available for publication. A few months later, after more communication, I received a copy of the notebook.

Woods, Shore, Desert: A Notebook, May 1968 begins with three quotes from the *Astavakra Gita,* following the direction of Merton's development.[4] Several Roman Catholic priests had written books suggesting a more ecumenical view of the world, but Merton was one of the few who were actually integrating the teachings of other religions into their spiritual disciplines, "reading the calligraphy of snow and rock." His teachers included Christian Desert Fathers, along with Taoist philosophers, Buddhist Zen Masters and Lamas, Hindu sadhus and Jewish Hasids. Here he returns "to sources," preparing to speak "of something new to which you might not yet have access."

On May 6 he flew from Louisville, via Chicago and San Francisco airports, to Eureka, California. Based at Our Lady of the Redwoods Monastery, Whitethorn, California, he ventured along the coast "with a small box of sun-kissed seedless raisins." Although still tentative, Merton is moving toward "an experiment in openness." Standing on the Pacific shore, looking hopefully to Asia, hearing the "faint cry of a lamb on the mountain side muffled by sea wind," breathing in the pungent world, breathing out the poetry of his vision . . . Bear Harbor, Needle Rock, Mattold Valley, wild irises "three or four feet high," calla lilies "growing wild among the ferns of a stream bank," roses, "and a lot of flowering shrubs that I cannot name." And always the redwoods "indescribably beautiful."

In 1963 John Howard Griffin asked Dom James Fox, Abbot of the Abbey of Gethsemani, if he could photograph Thomas Merton for a documentary archive. It was during the shooting session that Merton became interested in camera. According to Griffin, "The camera became in his hands, almost immediately, an instrument of contemplation."[5] "His concept of aesthetic beauty differed from that of most men. Most would pass by dead roots in search of a rose. Merton photographed the dead tree root or the texture of wood or whatever crossed his path . . . seeking not to alter their life but to prescrve it in his emulsions."[6] Not like Tennyson, who plucked the "flower in the crannied wall . . . roots and all." More like Ryokan, who wrote:

> The grasses of the garden,—
> They fall,
> And lie as they fall. [7]

Photography is a way of framing wholeness so that suchness reveals itself;[8] it "never makes the mistake of trying to turn from the material to the immaterial in hopes of conveying 'spirituality.' "[9] And Merton was a man of the earth. His eyes danced with shapes, textures, gestures of rock and woody plants; "illusions that are not normally admitted on the scene."[10] He was not a "photographer." For him, the camera was merely another tool "for dealing with things everybody knows about but isn't attending to."[11]

After a restless night in San Francisco, Merton flew to Albuquerque, New Mexico, the way to the Monastery of Christ in the Desert, 130 miles north of the city. He had published a collection of parables and sayings of the fourth-century Christian Desert Fathers;[12] but it is in his book *Thoughts in Solitude* that Merton most eloquently addresses contemporary problems in "the holy desert":

The desert Fathers believed that the wilderness had been created as supremely valuable in the eyes of God precisely because it had no value to men. The wasteland was the land that could never be wasted by men because it offered them nothing. There was nothing to attract them. There was nothing to exploit.

He goes on to lament:

When man and his money and machines move out into the desert, and dwell there, not fighting the devil as Christ did, but believing in his promise of power and wealth, and adoring his angelic wisdom, then the desert itself moves everywhere. Everywhere is desert. Everywhere is solitude in which man must do penance and fight the adversary and purify his own heart in the grace of God.[13]

Those words were written in the early morning gloom of Gethsemani. Now, motoring through the sunlight of New Mexico, there is the stark beauty of the Sangre de Cristo (Blood of Christ) Mountains, and "mesas, full rivers, cottonwoods, sagebrush, high red cliffs, piñon pines," and "miles of emptiness."

At the Monastery of Christ in the Desert, by day he walked up the canyon observing "a fat mountain ringed with pillared red cliffs, ponderous as the great Babylonian movie palaces of the 1920s, but far bigger." At night he awakened with stomach cramps and ran "barefooted down the cold pebble path to the hut with the toilet in it not knowing whether the toilet would flush."

What he was reading he wove into the fabric of what he was living. Thus "the curvature of space around *Mount Analogue*" is penetrated by "the calls of the crows in New Mexico" as he "pick(s) up the amice to begin to vest for concelebration." The connection. The path forever lengthening, the Vision approaching, " 'The Clear Light' and reality itself."[14]

This book would have been impossible to bring to publication without the encouragement, patience and research of Dr. Robert E. Daggy, Curator of the Merton Studies Center. I would also like to thank Br. Patrick Hart of the Abbey of Gethsemani; Fr. Blase Schauer of Liturgy in Santa Fe; Br. Brendan, Librarian, College of Santa Fe; Petrita Lara of the New Mexico State Library; Fr. Aelred Wall; Sister Veronique Geeroms of Redwoods Monastery; the Villagra

Book Shop; Br. Peter Buck, Br. Stephen Herman and Margaret West of Our Lady of Guadalupe Abbey, Pecos, New Mexico; and Denis Hines, W. H. Ferry, Peter Nabokov, Mary Worman, Robert and Priscilla Bunker, Alex Traube, and Craig Eyrich.

Joel Weishaus
Santa Fe, New Mexico

ITINERARY, May 1968

May 6:	Louisville, Kentucky to Chicago and San Francisco airports to Eureka, California
May 7-14:	Our Lady of the Redwoods Monastery, Whitethorn, California, with short side trips
May 15:	To San Francisco, California
May 16:	To Albuquerque, New Mexico
May 17:	To Monastery of Christ in the Desert, Abiquiu, New Mexico
May 20:	Albuquerque, New Mexico to Memphis, Tennessee to Louisville, Kentucky

Based on a compilation by Dr. Robert E. Daggy and Br. Patrick Hart.

WOODS, SHORE, DESERT

PRELUDE

Points for Conferences.

"The wiseman who has known the truth of the self plays the game of life and there is no similarity between his way of living and the deluded who live in the world as mere beasts of burden."

Astavakra Gita

"Where there is I, there is bondage. Where there is no I, there is release. Neither reject nor accept anything."

Astavakra Gita

"Whether he lives a life of action or withdraws from the world, the ignorant man does not find spiritual peace."

Astavakra Gita

"Orthodoxy is the principle of absolute freedom."

Yelchaninov

The fear of placing rules, thoughts, and words above the fact or outside the fact, this fear is important in Orthodoxy, is the basis of the freedom of the Orthodox.

Aversion to propaganda, to indoctrination and to undue restraints: Orthodoxy, says Yelchaninov, means "putting our whole faith in the actual presence of religious life and all the rest will come of itself."

Three dreams of Descartes are central in his philosophy. They have a religious importance. The God of Descartes is absolute reality, timeless, simple, instantaneous action, breaking through into the conscious like a thunder clap.

Port Royal.
Return to sources.
Vernacular use of Bible and the Fathers. Emphasis on redemption and grace. Emphasis on liberty or a more flexible idea of authority. They were ruined by the authoritarians.
The Jansenism of the end of the 17th century was something different. It was merely anti-Jesuit. Yes, they were pessimistic. Yes, they were combative. This is an example of a debate which made everybody wrong.

The priest, Monsieur De Sainte Martre, he went sneaking out from Paris by night along the wall of Port Royal to a tree which he climbed and from which he gave conferences to the nuns inside. Of this Sainte Beuve says: "Voilà presque du scabreux, ce me semble; voilà les balcons nocturnes de Port Royal!"
The serenades!

The nocturnal balconies of California.

Brother rather than father. Partnership in seeking to understand our monastic vocation.

A happening.

Presence and witness but also speaking of the unfamiliar . . . speaking of something new to which you might not yet have access.

An experiment in openness.

Problems.

Too much conformity to roles. Is it just a matter of brushing up the roles and adjusting the roles? A role is not necessarily a vocation. One can be alienated by role filling.

Background.

Nazareth, Beguines, mystics of the Rhineland, beginning of the modern consciousness.

Problems.

Contemplative mystique. Feminine mystique. Theology of vows. Monastic life as an eschatological sign. Risk and hope. The promise of God to the poor or the promises of the beast to the rich? Judgement of power. Ecclesiastical power. Power prevents renewal. Power prevents real change. Garments of skins in the Greek fathers. Hindu Kosas, then modern consciousness. Montaigne, Descartes, Pascal, Sufis, and Zen.

Astavakra Gita.

Christ consciousness in N.T.

Pascal said, "It is the joy of having found God which is the source of the sorrow of having offended Him."

Pascal said, "He is not found except by the ways taught by the Gospel. He is not preserved except by the ways taught in the Gospel.

Thou wouldst not seek Me if thou hadst not already found Me. (St. Bernard, Pascal.)

Of Pascal, Poulet says, "Lived time is for Pascal as it had been for St. Augustine! The present of an immediate consciousness in which appear and combine themselves with it retrospective and prospective movements which give to that present an amplitude and a *boundless temporal density.*"

Words of Martin Luther King, recently shot, copied on the plane.

He said: "So I say to you, seek God and discover Him and make Him a power in your life. Without Him all our efforts turn to ashes and our sunrises to darkest nights."

May 6th

O'Hare, big fish with tail fins elevated in light smog.

One leaves earth.

"Not seeing, he appears to see." *Astavakra Gita*

Snow covered mountains. Thirty-nine thousand feet over Idaho.

Frozen lakes. Not a house, not a road. Gulfs. No announcement. Hidden again.

We are all secrets. But now, where there are suggested gaps, one can divine rocks and snow. "Be a mountain diviner!"

Whorled dark profile of a river in snow. A cliff in the fog. And now a dark road straight through a long fresh snow field. Snaggy reaches of snow pattern. Claws of mountain and valley. Light shadow of breaking cloud on snow. Swing and reach of long, gaunt, black, white forks.

The new consciousness.

Reading the calligraphy of snow and rock from the air.

A sign of snow on a mountainside as if my own ancestors were hailing me.

We bump. We burst into secrets.

Blue shadowed mountains and woods under the cloud, then tiny shinings, tin roofed houses at a crossroad. An olive-green valley floor. A low ridge thinly picked out at the very top in blown snow. The rest, deep green. One of the most lovely calligraphies I have ever seen. Distant inscaped mountains and near flat lowland. A scrawl of long fire. Smoke a mile or two long. Then a brown rich-veined river. A four lane super highway with nothing on it.

Utah? It's dry.

Far down, a bright nosed armed jet goes by very fast.

Six thousand dead sheep.

Utah. Something I saw shining alone in a valley a moment ago could have been our monastery.

"New secret poison gas harms no one but the enemy."

Six thousand dead sheep.

Over the Nevada desert, nothing.

A long compacted serpent of cloud running north-south dominates, presides over the other looser clouds floating below relaxed, flaccid, and abandoned, flying slowly from west to east.

Six thousand dead sheep.

Real desert, not snow.

Salt.

A copper mine:

Red involved shamanic sign inscribed on the flat waste.

A sign of a stream ending in nothing. Pure dead, unsigned flats. Nada!

San Francisco. Two daiquiris in the airport bar. Impression of relaxation. Even only in the airport, a sense of recovering something of myself that has been long lost.

8

On the little plane to Eureka, the same sense of ease, of openness. Sense of relaxation while waiting because this is a different land, a different country, a more South American or Central American city. Significant?

A. Stern says of Sartre, "Each philosopher can only give the truth of his own existence. That is to say, philosophy is not a universal or impersonal science. Each individual perspective requires the others as its complements. The Existentialist's world view is determined by his actions and his means of action."

Unamuno said, "Philosophy is a product of each philosopher and each philosopher is a man of flesh and blood, who addresses himself to other men of flesh and blood like himself and whatever he may do, he does not philosophize with his reason alone but with his will, his feeling, his flesh and blood, with his whole soul and his whole body. It is the whole man who philosophizes in us."

Contrast Hegel, who said, "The teaching of philosophy is precisely what frees man from the endless crowd of finite aims and intentions by making him so indifferent to them that their existence or non-existence is to him a matter of no moment."

Consistency.

Is the pseudomonastic experience an attempt to convince ourselves that we are somehow necessary? . . . Justification by monastic works or by a metaphysical consciousness?

Sartre said of the *Salauds,* "They tried to overcome their contingency by inventing a necessary being."

Monastic discipline: Learning to exist as a subject without a world? Primacy of the conscious subject, creating a certain consciousness to justify our existence instead of appreciating the primacy of existence as concrete, subjective, given, not to be acquired!
Fatal emphasis (in a monastic life) on acquiring something. What about this imperative? Does it make sense? "Convince yourself that you exist!" Baloney!

May 7th

It was quiet flying to Eureka yesterday afternoon in a half empty plane. One jet flight a day to this forgotten lumber town. Distant presences of Lassen peak and Mount Shasta, especially Shasta . . . like great silent Mexican gods, white and solemn. Massively suspended alone, over haze and over thousands of lower ridges.

The redwood lands appear. Even from the air you can see that the trees are huge. And from the air too, you can see where the hillsides have been slashed into, ravaged, sacked, stripped, eroded with no hope of regrowth of these marvelous trees.

We land in Eureka, a windy, vacant field by the ocean. Vast sea, like lead, with a cold steady, humid wind blowing off it . . . almost as if there were no town at all; a few low wooden buildings, and a palm tree, and rhododendron in bloom. I see Sister Leslie and Father Roger at the gate. Sister compliments me on wearing a beret.

Eureka, a curious low town of wooden buildings—strange leaden light. It is a fine day for Eureka. You can see the sun. Most of the time it is hidden in fog.

Signs.

A baroque yellow and black Victorian mansion which I five times photographed.

The place strangely reminds me of Little Neck, Long Island or maybe Alaska, or maybe Siberia, . . . God knows. The strange desolate windy low slung non-town, yet with stores. We get a couple of cans of beer.

Driving down through the redwoods was indescribably beautiful along Eel River. There is one long stretch where the big trees have been protected and saved—like a completely primeval forest. Everything from the big ferns at the base of the trees, the dense undergrowth, the long enormous shafts towering endlessly in shadow penetrated here and there by light. A most moving place—like a cathedral. I kept thinking of the notes of Francis Ponge on the fir forest of Central France. But what could one say about *these*?

May 13th

I am on the Pacific Shore—perhaps fifty miles south of Cape Mendocino. Wide open, deserted hillside frequented only by sheep and swallows, sun and wind. No people for miles either way. Breakers on the black sand. Crying gulls fly down and land neatly on their own shadows.

I am half way between Needle Rock, where there is an abandoned house, and Bear Harbor, where there is another abandoned house—3 miles between them. No human habitation in sight on all the miles of shore line either way, though there is a small sheep ranch hidden beyond Needle Rock.

North, toward Shelter Cove, a manufactory of clouds where the wind piles up smoky moisture along the steep flanks of the mountains. Their tops are completely hidden.

Back inland, in the Mattole Valley at the convent, it is probably raining.

South, bare twin pyramids. And down at the shore, a point of rock on which there is a silent immobile convocation of seabirds, perhaps pelicans.

Far out at sea, a long low coastal vessel seems to get nowhere. It hangs in an isolated patch of light like something in eternity.

And yet, someone has been here before me with a small box of sun-kissed seedless raisins and I too have one of these. So this other may have been a nun from the redwoods.

A huge shark lolls in the swells making his way southward, close in shore, showing his dorsal fin.

Faint cry of a lamb on the mountain side muffled by sea wind.

When I came four or five days ago to Needle Rock, I told the rancher I would be out on this mountainside for a few days. He had just finished shearing. All the sheep were still penned in at the ranch. Now they are all over the mountain again.

This morning I sheltered under a low thick pine while sheep stood bare and mute in the pelting shower.

Song sparrows everywhere in the twisted trees—"Neither accept or reject anything." *Astavakra Gita*

Low tide. Long rollers trail white sleeves of foam behind them, reaching for the sand, like hands for the keyboard of an instrument.

May 14th

Sister Katryn danced barefoot in the choir Sunday after Mass. Beauty of these Flemish nuns and of the American nuns too. More beautiful in their simple blue and gray dresses without veils than in the affected and voluminous Cistercian habit—the cowl and choker. But they wear light cowls in choir and can wear such veils as they please. Some, like the chantress, a dignified mantilla. Others, a headband, others, nothing.

I told them I wanted to ask my Abbot's permission to spend Lent in

the abandoned house at Needle Rock. Sister Dominique said they would all fight one another for the chance to bring me supplies.

Yesterday afternoon, late, waiting by the small barn with gray, well weathered redwood shingles. The calm ocean with high cumulus clouds reflected in it and swallows circling the barn in the sunny air.

Not to run from one thought to the next, says Theophane the Recluse, but to give each one time to settle in the heart.

Attention. Concentration of the spirit in the
　　heart.
Vigilance. Concentration of the will in the
　　heart.
Sobriety. Concentration of feeling in the
　　heart.

Bear Harbor is in many ways better than Needle Rock—more isolated, more sheltered. A newer house, in better repair, with a generator. You reach it finally after barns, and the tall eucalyptus grove.

Flowers at Bear Harbor. Besides wild irises three or four feet high, there are calla lilies growing wild among the ferns on the stream bank. A profusion of roses and a lot of flowering shrubs that I cannot name.

Bear Harbor—rocky cove piled up with driftwood logs, some of which have been half burned. Much of it could serve for firewood.

When Father Roger drove me out here this morning, it was low tide. Four cars or trucks were parked by the old dead tree at Needle Rock and people were fishing for abalone. Two other cars met us on the road as we went down. That's too many.

There were even two cars at Bear Harbor and two pairs of young men . . . one of them a teacher interested in Zen.

About a mile from Bear Harbor, there is a hollow in which I am now sitting, where one could comfortably put a small trailer. A small loud

stream, many quail.

The calm ocean . . . very blue through the trees. Calla lilies growing wild. A very active flycatcher. The sun shines through his wings as through a Japanese fan. It is the feast of St. Pachomius. Many ferns. A large unfamiliar hawktype bird flew over a little while ago, perhaps a young eagle.

I called Ping Ferry in Santa Barbara last evening. He spoke of birds, of the shore, of Robinson Jeffers and told me the name of the big jay bird all dark-blue with a black crest which I saw yesterday. It is called Stellers Jay. Does the jay know whose bird he is? I doubt it. A marvelous blue!

My piece on the "Wild Places" is to be printed in the *Center Magazine*.

Two ailing lombardy poplars, an ancient picket fence among the thistles: there must have been a house here once. Behind me a high wall of wooded mountain, green firs with many solitary, burned masts standing out above them. Wild fox gloves by the stream just where it sings loudest.

Yesterday, when Father Roger came to pick me up, he brought the mail. Most of it useless. There was a letter from Naomi Burton who said that the *Journal of my Escape from the Nazis* passes from hand to

hand at Doubleday and nobody knows what to make of it.

Lecture edifiante. The Russian priest Sylvester wrote a famous book called the *Domostroy.* This Sylvester was the advisor of Ivan the Terrible but before he became terrible, so says the author I am reading. Domostroy seems to be the Russian equivalent of *Good Housekeeping.* Good housekeeping for a Tzar whose housekeeping is not yet terrible.

Eugene Popov, honorary member of the Ecclesiastical Academy of St. Petersburg, taught that it was "a sin to make the sign of the cross with gloves on."

I wonder about the definition of Orthodoxy as hostility to rules worked out by Yelchaninov and quoted at the beginning. I wonder.

Eight crows wheel in the sky. An interesting evolution of shadows on the bare hillside beneath them. Sometimes the crows fly low and their dance mingles with the dance of their own shadows on the almost perpendicular olive wall of the mountain pasture. Below, the sighs of the ocean.

"How many incarnations hast thou devoted to the actions of body, mind and speech? They have brought thee nothing but pain. Why not cease from them?" *Astavakra Gita*

Reincarnation or not, I am as tired of talking and writing as if I had done it for centuries. Now it is time to listen at length to this Asian ocean. Over there, Asia.

Yesterday, in this place, looking southwest, I thought of New Zealand and the *Wahine* and my Aunt Kit getting into the last lifeboat. It capsized.

I was sitting in the shade near the spot where the jay cried out on the branch over my head yesterday and awakened me as I was dozing in the sun. A red pick-up truck came up the dirt road. The owner of the land was in it with his wife and said he would be willing to rent me his house at Bear Harbor if plans work out for him in September but he can't commit himself until then.

May 16th

I am flying over snowy mountains towards Las Vegas and Albuquerque and I read Han Yu's versatilities about mountains in the book of late *T'ang* poems I got yesterday at City Lights.

The snow suddenly gives place to a copper colored desert.

We drove down together this time yesterday from Thorn. Mother Myriam is going reluctantly to the Chapter of Abbesses at Citeaux. Sister Katryn drove. Al Groth, the neighbor, with the Heineken's beer rode in the back seat. I cashed Dan Walsh's check at Garberville together with another small royalty on the Bellarmine book, the symposium about the Council.

Eel River Valley. Redwoods. Redwood tourist traps, but also real groves. After lunch at Ukiah we went among fruit growing towns, old brown wineries, conservative Cloverdale with a few oranges still in the trees and signs saying, "Impeach Earl Warren" and "Don't sell anything to the Reds."

Below, now, Death Valley.

At Santa Rosa, four gamblers were yelling in a cool Hofbrau. Draft Löwenbraü! Then we went to a place for prescriptions by the hospital. Then off on the bright freeway to the city.

The fine wide ranches, low white houses, eucalyptus, pepper wood, pine, fruit trees. We crossed the Golden Gate bridge in bright sunlight, the whole city clear.

A man, chased in vain by a painter who wanted to prevent him, had jumped off the bridge about an hour before.

Downtown San Francisco. I walked about a bit while the sisters went to find Portia, their postulant with whom they were to stay. Portia was getting off work at Penneys.

I called Ferlinghetti. I went first to City Lights but he was not there. I got the T'ang poets, Heilo, something on Zen, William Carlos Williams, "Kora in Hell." We had supper at an Italian restaurant, Polos. Ferlinghetti came after we had finished the bottle of Chianti. I went off with him to an Espresso place on Grant Avenue, the Trieste, where a young musician told of some visions he had had. Good visions, and not on drugs either.

Below, completely arid rocks, valley floor streaked with salt, bone dry. Twenty minutes from Las Vegas.

Turbulence at lower altitudes, we hear.

"And some, like champions, Fen or Yü,
When the stakes are down, eager for the prize ahead,
The foremost and strongest rearing high above . . .
The losers looking foolish and speechless with rage."
In the little Italian restaurant in the North Beach area where I had an early breakfast today, a Chinese man, looking as though bewildered with drugs or something, ate repeated orders of macaroni with bottles of beer. It was seven o'clock in the morning. Much comment in Italian by the staff and the patrons. One of the hatted Italians whirled his finger next to his temple and pointed to the man, "you're crazy."

"I fear that heaven, just like man can lose its sight by lusting after beauty." Lu T'ung

We bump down into Las Vegas over burned red and ochre canyons. Interesting rock peaks—like Sinai. Turbulence.

I stayed overnight last night at City Lights publications offices. A bedroom with a mattress on the floor, a guitar and a tape recorder and a window opening on a fire escape—a block from the top of Telegraph Hill. Noise of cars roaring up the steep streets all night. Finally it got quiet about 1:30. I think I slept from 2 to 5 and also an hour somewhere around midnight.

Morning. Lovely little Chinese girls going in all directions to school, one with a violin.

A wide meteorite crator in the Arizona desert, like a brown and red morning glory.

I am the utter poverty of God. I am His emptiness, littleness, nothingness, lostness. When this is understood, my life in His freedom, the self-emptying of God in me is the fullness of grace. A love for God that knows no reason because He is the fullness of grace. A love for God that knows no reason because He is God; a love without measure, a love for God as personal. The Ishvara appears as personal in order to inspire this love. Love for all, hatred of none is the fruit and manifestation of love for God—peace and satisfaction. Forgetfulness of worldly pleasure, selfishness and so on in the love for God, channeling all passion and emotion into the love for God.

Technology as Karma.

What can be done has to be done. The burden of possibility that has to be fulfilled, possibilities which demand so imperatively to be fulfilled that everything else is sacrificed for their fulfillment.

Computer Karma in American civilization.

Distinguish work as narcotic (that is being an operator and all that goes with it), from healthy and free work.

But also consider the wrong need for non-action. The *Astavakra Gita* says: "Do not let the fruit of action be your motive and do not be attached to non-action." In other words, do not let your left hand know what your right hand is doing. Work to please God alone.

Krishna says in the *Bhagavad Gita,* "By devotion in work He knows me, knows what in truth I am and who I am. Then having known me in truth, He enters into me.

The states of life. *Brahmacharya.* The life of the student in chastity under his Guru. *Grhastha.* The life of the householder begetting children, practicing Karma Yoga. *Vanaprastha.* The forest life. My present life. A life of privacy and of quasiretirement. Is there one more stage? Yes. *Sanyasa.* Total renunciation. Homelessness, begging. The *Sanyasin* lives only on food given to him. He is freed from all ritual obligations. The sacred fire is kindled only within. No household shrine. No temple. He is entirely turned to deliverance, has renounced all activity and attachment, all fear, all greed, all care, without home, without roof, without place, without name, without office, without function, without reputation, without care for reputation, without being known.

May 17th

I am at the Monastery of Christ in the Desert, Abiquiu, New Mexico. I was bombarded by impressions getting here yesterday. The vast sweep of the Rio Grande Valley.

Sangre de Cristo Mountains, blue and snowy.

But after Santa Fe, marvelous long line of snowless, arid mountains, clean long shapes stretching for miles under pure light. Mesas, full rivers, cottonwoods, sagebrush, high red cliffs, piñon pines. Most impressed of all by the miles of emptiness.

This monastery is thirteen miles by dirt road from the nearest highway. In that distance, only one other house is passed—Skull Ranch. Around the monastery, nothing. Perfect silence. Bright stars at night dimly light the guest room. The only noise the puttering of the pilot light in the gas heater. The adobe building is full of beautiful Santos, old ones and new ones, serious as painted desert birds.

New Mexican workman on the lovely chapel whose roof recently began to leak. It has to be redone.

Nakashima's placing of the chapel: working its lines into the setting

of cliffs, is great. Inexhaustible interest of the building from all angles and in all lights. It is the best monastic building in the country.

There are only two monks here now; Dom Aelred, the founder, and Father Gregory. Both from the founding group at Mount Saviour. They were previously at Portsmouth Priory. There is also a hermit, Father Denis, a Cistercian from Snowmass in Colorado whom I have not yet seen.

"All blue is precious," said a friend of Gertrude Stein. There is very much of it here. A fortune in clear sky and the air . . . so good it almost knocked me down when I got off the plane in Albuquerque.

Father Roger, at the Redwoods, could not pronounce Albuquerque.

Alone, amid red rocks, small pine and cedar, facing the high wall on the other side of the Chama canyon. But east, the view opens out on distant mountains beyond the wider valley where the monastery is.

Light and shadow on the wind erosion patterns of the rocks. Silence except for the gull-like, questioning crys of jays.

Distant sound of muddy rushing water in the Chama River below me. I could use up rolls of film on nothing but these rocks. The whole canyon replete with emptiness.

"When the mind is stirred and perceives things before it as objects of thought, it will find in itself something lacking." *Astavakra Gita*

To find this "something lacking" is already a beginning of wisdom.

Ignorance seeks to make good the "lacking" with better or more complete or more mysterious objects. The lack itself will be complete as void.

Not to deny subject and object but to realize them as void.

The alleluia antiphon for Terce at the Redwoods Monastery, composed by Sister Dominique, stays with me and is associated with the monastery . . .

The young redwoods clustered outside the big window of the chapel and then the ocean, Needle Rock and Bear Harbor.

The sun on the vast water, the sound of the waves. Yet the sound of the wind in the piñon pines here is very much the same.

The liturgy at the Redwoods was excellent. I enjoyed the daily concelebration with Father Roger, with the nuns coming up to stand around close to the altar at the end of the offertory and one of them extinguishing the candles as they retired after communion.

I have not yet concelebrated here at Christ in the Desert. That is to be this evening when I go back from the canyon to the monastery. In spite of the cedars and piñon pines, this is real desert in which one could well get lost among boulders, except that the end of the canyon is well in sight.

Just as in California around Thorn, I could see hollows and valleys like those of Kentucky, so here the view out at the end of the canyon is something like that from my own hermitage . . . a straight line of dark green hills with hollows and open patches. Only here, there is also a red wall of cliff and it is all much higher and the air is much clearer.

For the first time since I have been away, I now have the feeling that I might be glad to get back to Kentucky, but not to mail and visitors and invitations that I will have to refuse and other things that I will not be able to avoid.

A gang of gray jays flies down into the canyon with plaintive cat-like cries over my head. Some stop to question my presence. They reply to one another all over the canyon. They would rob me if they thought I had anything worthwhile. Gray Jay, "Whiskey Jack," a camp robber, inquisitive, versatile (says the bird book).

May 18th

When I got in from my day in the canyon yesterday, after passing the goat barn and reaching the adobe building of the monastery guest house, I saw Father Gregory with some people and he introduced me to Don Devereux and his wife . . . Ping Ferry's friends from Santa Fe. There was much talk of Indians at supper.

Today in Don's old truck, we went to Abiquiu. I mailed 6 rolls of film to John Griffin to develop and we drove around the plaza . . . saw the adobe walls of Georgia O'Keeffe's house, the garden full of vegetation. Then, down the road, the site of the old pueblo that Don knew about, and two shrines. The site was superb, high over the valley, and one could imagine something of the way it was in the ancient civilization. The east opening of the shrine toward distant snow-covered mountains where obviously the sun rises at the June equinox. I came away with pockets full of pottery fragments and a tiny, almost entire obsidian arrowhead, like black glass.

I have run out of black and white film and had to get color film in Abiquiu. I took pictures of a lot of odd volcanic rocks lying around on Ghost Ranch. Vast sprinklers were watering the alfalfa and the lawns, neat houses of the Presbyterians, conference rooms and so forth of this religious center.

Don was telling me about the Alianza and Tijerina, an attack on a courthouse and a murder. Tijerina fled to the mountains and was interviewed secretly in his mountain hideout by Peter Nabokov, the young newspaper man whose book on the Indians I reviewed.

Simmering unrest in all this area. People set fire secretly to the government forest. There is much resentment about the land being taken from them . . . land which was granted to their ancestors by the Spanish crown.

Mexicans are working on the damaged church at Christ in the Desert and there is a water problem there.

I got up in the middle of the night with stomach cramps and ran barefoot down the cold pebble path to the hut with the toilet in it not knowing whether the toilet would flush. Fortunately, it did.

Arsenio, the Indian cook, makes fine breakfast for the workmen.

Father Aelred bought some beer the other day and Arsenio drank up a whole case of it in one night.

This morning I began looking at the copy of Daumal's *Mount Analogue,* which Ferlinghetti just published and which he gave me in San Francisco.

Up the canyon from where I now sit, a couple of miles below the monastery, there is the heavy, domed architecture of a fat mountain ringed with pillared red cliffs, ponderous as the great Babylonian movie palaces of the 1920s, but far bigger.

Fresh wind, song of an ordinary robin in the low gnarled cedars.

May 19th

Fifth Sunday after Easter.

From *Mount Analogue:* "How it was proved that a hitherto unknown continent really existed with mountains much higher than the Himalaya . . . how it happened that no one detected it before . . . how we reached it, what creatures we met there—how another expedition pursuing quite different goals, barely missed destruction."

Last night at dusk, the three tame white ducks went running very fast through the green alfalfa to the river, plunging into the swift waters, swimming to the other side, standing up in the shallows, flapping their white wings. Then the fourth discovered their absence and followed them through another corner of the alfalfa field.

The calls of the crows here in New Mexico as in California, are more muted, more melodious, briefer, less insistant than in the east. The crows seem to be flying at a greater psychic altitude, in a different realm. Yes, of course, a realm of high rocks and stunted piñon pine.

The curvature of space around *Mount Analogue* makes it possible for people to live as though Mount Analogue did not exist. Hence, everyone comes from an unknown country and almost everyone from a too well-known country.

Georgia O'Keeffe did not come to the monastery to lunch today since she had to wait at her house at Abiquiu for a framer. Others came. Peter Nabokov, and so forth. We ate a large salad in the hot sun. I went quickly to rest afterwards to escape conversation.

This morning I had a long and rather funny talk with Father Denis at his fieldstone hermitage by the river. He has a nice red cat. We talked of the Cistercian Order and of the monasteries and people in it—a discouraging topic.

May 20th

Evening. Sun setting over Memphis Airport. I have come in a slow prop plane over flooded Arkansas country from Dallas. Between Albuquerque and Dallas, I finished *Mount Analogue,* a very fine book.

It ends at a strange moment, a sign for the eschatological conscience
. . . or it does not end, for the climb has only begun.

Peter Nabokov came to the monastery in the afternoon yesterday. I
was glad to meet him and talk to him. There was much to say about
the Poor People's March, for he had been at a demonstration in
Albuquerque the day before. He said Albuquerque was very sweet
. . . sweet, he meant, to the poor people.

May 22

All the time in the Chama canyon, I was looking out for rattlesnakes. It
is full of sidewinders. I went gingerly among the rocks and looked
everywhere before sitting down. I thought they would like best the
heat of the day and the burning rocks, but Denis said they preferred
dusk, evening, and the night, yet, the nights are cold. In the end, I saw
no rattlers except at the zoo in Ghost Ranch Museum. There, a huge
ugly monster of a diamondback and three indescribably beautiful
others, whose name I forgot . . . long, lithe, silvery, sandy snakes with
neat rattles lifting up their heads gracefully with swollen sacks of
poison. They were too beautiful, too alive, too much themselves to
be labeled, still less to have an emotion, fear, admiration, or surprise
projected on them. You would meet one in the rocks and hardly see it
for it would be so much like the silver, dead, weathered cedar branches
lying everywhere and exactly the color of sand or of desert vegetation. I
understand the Indians' respect for the snake—so different from the
attitude ingrained in us since Genesis—our hatred and contempt.

In the desert one does not fight snakes, one simply lives with them
and keeps out of their way.

The buildings of San Francisco, the two-spired church in North
Beach, the apartments and streets of Telegraph Hill in warm, pale,
South American or desert colors . . . snake colors, but charming and
restful. Pretty as Havana and less noisy, though there was plenty of
motor noise at night with cars climbing those steep hills.

Poulet says, "The starting point of the comic art of Molière is situated in the occasion in which a being is comprehended only through his actions." A demeanor, proper to an occasion, a basis of judgement, for instance: "This is a flying doctor." How do you know? He has a stethoscope. He flies. He is a non-conformist.

Picture of South African heart transplant patient passing a ball to international rugby players, who grin. When will we know if his heart now beats differently for his old wife? It is a Negro heart! Comedy: demeanor and *mis*demeanor!

A demeanor is therefore a misdemeanor. A misdemeanor in another is a cause of satisfaction to one whose own demeanor is not missing. We are not accustomed to seeing gentlemen act like this: which proves that we ourselves are gentlemen. (Not flying doctors or heart transplants with Negro hearts.) Until such time as the very fact of being a gentleman itself becomes ridiculous.

He is no menace to existence, clinging to a vanished order! Only the menace is to be taken seriously.

The gentleman is funny! And long-haired students sit in the office of Grayson Kirk at Columbia smoking his cigars as if they liked cigars. But then, you see, the gentleman can also eventually call the police, thereby re-establishing some claim to reality, and it is the long hairs who are now funny (in jail?).

Thus says Poulet, "The comic is the perception of an ephemeral and local fracture in the middle of a durable and normal world." Well, that remains to be seen.

"Let the painter come to terms with his impatience." Words of Molière on The Painter of Frescoes and the comic playwright. Nominalism of Molière. Repeated hammering on one point until the character is depersonalized, generalized: *"miser! miser! miser!"* This is also the art of torture in the police state. To repeat an accusation until it sticks and the accused is both generalized and objectivized by pain.

To "make an example of."

"Now the soul is pleased when it *makes an example* of somebody else." Words of Poulet. "It will renew in itself the idea of the very lively pleasure it tasted that first time." Comedy is indeed close to torture!

And the French are now perhaps succeeding in making an example of DeGaulle who first of all, made an example of himself.

"Par exemple!," the two meanings—*qui peut servir de modèle* or *chatiment qui peut servir de leçon.*

But De Gaulle was always the pure exclamation, the *par exemple!* with the kepi on his head, who the other day exclaimed (as I saw in the San Francisco paper): *"La reforme, oui; le chienlit, non!"*

Somewhere, when I was in some plane or in some canyon, Dan

and Phil Berrigan and some others took A-1 draft files from a draft center in a Baltimore suburb and burned them in a parking lot. Somewhere I heard they were arrested but I've seen no paper and don't know anything, but an envelope came from Dan with a text of a preface to his new book, evidently on the Hanoi trip, saying he was going to do this. It was mailed from Baltimore, May 17th, and had scrawled on it, "Wish us luck."

John Griffin sent one of my pictures of Needle Rock, which he developed and enlarged. I also have the contact. The Agfa film brought out the great *Yang-Yin* of sea rock mist, diffused light and half hidden mountain . . . an interior landscape, yet there. In other words, what is written within me is there. "Thou art that."

I dream every night of the west.

May 30th

The country which is nowhere is the real home; only it seems that the Pacific Shore at Needle Rock is more nowhere than this, and Bear Harbor is more nowhere still. (I was tempted to cross that out but in these notes, I am leaving everything, permitting everything.)

And are you there, my dears? Still under the big trees, going about your ways and your tasks, up the steep slope to the roomy wooden place where the chasubles are woven . . . Sister Gerarda on a bicycle to the guest quarters, Sister William to bake hosts, big warm Sister Veronica in the kitchen, Sister Katryn to be an obscure descendent of Eckhart's Sister Katrei. Sister Katryn and Sister Christofora were the ones who seemed to respond the most knowingly whenever Eckhart was mentioned.

Sister Dominique, the impulsive, the blue dressed, the full of melodies, who drove me in the car to the store to buy levis; big gentle Sister Leslie from Vassar and blue-eyed Sister Diane from Arizona interested in Ashrams and Sister Shalom and Sister Cecilia, who came later to the party . . . and Mother Myriam, the Abbess, was responsible for this wonderful place. Which ones have I forgotten besides the two

postulants, small dark Carol with the Volkswagen and big Portia from San Francisco?

Near the monastery, the tall silent redwoods, the house of the Looks and another house, neighbors by the Mattole River. The county line: here Mendocino, there Humboldt. My desolate shore is Mendocino. I must return.

The convicts came in an olive drab bus to cut brush along the roadside by the guest house. Smoking remains of green bonfires all along the limits of Al Groth's place. I did not see the convicts working—I was at the empty shore that day. I returned only after they were gone.

As we approached Sausalito, on the highway to San Francisco, someone pointed out San Quentin as the place where the convicts came from. A sinister white building on the bay.

Again I remember the Hofbrau outside Santa Rosa—the German Hofbrau in a wide Mexican valley by the American super highway. We took the wrong turn, got in the wrong parking lot, then out again into the right parking lot. The nuns waited in the car.

All around the hospital in Santa Rosa, the low offices of the gynecologists.

When I came, the convicts were cutting brush five miles northeast of Thorn. When I left, they were working and leaving bonfires near the monastery. Father Roger said: "they will not cross the stream."

I remember the desk smelling of oranges and my money in the top left-hand drawer in the old Bond Street wallet my guardian gave me on my 18th birthday before I started for the Riviera and Italy.

The narrow shower and the waste can full of orange peels, squeezed grapefruit, the sponge on the wash basin, the bed heavy with dreams, the window curtain that pulled the wrong way, the dish of fruit on the bedroom table, the broken vase of roses replaced by field flowers, mail to go in a cardboard box in the utility room of unit one, mail read and thrown in the waste baskets smelling of oranges. Instant coffee at 4:30 a.m. with the Japanese coil—Do not touch for a few seconds after.

In the earthenware mug—"mug," I tell Father Roger, "not a cup, a *mug.*"

Yogi and the cats. He fought them over his meat. He let them have his milk. Yogi used to belong to Diane. She asked about Ashrams, Diane!

Yogi romping over from unit one across the grass in the mist. I am going to the end of Lauds and to the whole-wheat bread and coffee and breakfast.

The long low monastery—its significance in the mist—chimneys— ventilators, like gray signs—the tops of the redwoods lost in the mist.

Chickens in the evening roosting in a line on a branch over the drinking fountain. No use.

Water in the drums of gasoline. Loggers explain to Father Roger as they siphon rust out of his engine—We do not go driving into the hills, drops of rust on the dusty ground.

I told them Sidi Abdesalam (the Sufi from Morocco) had asked me about my dreams, about my Abbot, and had said, "Within a year, there will be some change." And indeed, there was a change—for the better.

Then I arrived back here in Kentucky in all this rain. The small hardwoods are full of green leaves but are they real trees?

The worshipful cold spring light on the sandbanks of Eel River, the immense silent redwoods. Who can see such trees and bear to be away from them? I must go back. It is not right that I should die under lesser trees.

While I was coming back, the students at Columbia were flying the Viet Cong flag over each building and each building had its own commune.

Leslie knew the name of every flower between Eureka and the monastery.

Cold spring light on the sandbanks of Eel River. Communes, gasoline drums, burned stumps of the redwood trees big enough for houses. I told them in the store I came from Kentucky and they were pleased. Not so, in the airport bar. There is no point in living ten miles from Jim Beam. Who needs Kentucky?

Rain. Work. Talk. Meetings. And a curfew on rioting Louisville.

End of Terce. I walk into the sacristy listening for the lovely Alleluias of Dominique. I leave the door half open. The nuns' voices, the tall trees outside the big window. The mysterious sky above the frosted skylight. I pick up the amice to begin to vest for concelebration.

Putting it all back after Mass. The folded altar-cloths in the drawer, the table. Diane walking outside the enormous window, looked up into the sunlight and seemed happy.

Climbing to the top of the high ridge before the sea: tall firs reaching into the sun above smokes, mists. Then down into the ferns!

I drove back with Gracie. We met the logger at a crossing in his white helmet in his pickup. Therefore Father Roger's truck broke down Thursday because this was the day after.

Looking down from the steep height, I saw Gracie, very small, very far, carrying her blanket from the dead tree to the car.

Winifred, her spring painting, a larva or fetus inspiring white reeds.

As we climbed the steep road, Winifred's hair was wet and stringy as if she had been swimming. And I opened letters.

Gracie told me about her son and his school. One of the little white bastards wrote "nigger" in the toilet. Others told her son they were sorry such a thing could happen in San Rafael.

The towhee in the wet Kentucky wood. Void. Nightfall. My meetings are temporarily over.

Hisamatsu: natural, rational and Zen spontaneity. "This is true self," he says, "going beneath spontaneity."

Hisamatsu also says, "There is a big difference between the ultimate self and the self discussed in psychology. When one reaches ultimate self, spontaneity is changed into ultimate spontaneity. Zen spontaneity comes from ultimate self . . . formless self which is never occupied with any form." And he adds, "In western music, great silence is not found."

In our monasticism, we have been content to find our way to a kind of peace, a simple undisturbed thoughtful life. And this is certainly good, but is it good enough?

I, for one, realize that now I need more. Not simply to be quiet, somewhat productive, to pray, to read, to cultivate leisure—*otium sanctum!* There is a need of effort, deepening, change and transformation. Not that I must undertake a special project of self-transformation or that I must "work on myself." In that regard, it would be better to forget it. Just to go for walks, live in peace, let change come quietly and invisibly on the inside.

But I do have a past to break with, an accumulation of inertia, waste, wrong, foolishness, rot, junk, a great need of clarification of mindfulness, or rather of no mind—a return to genuine practice, right effort, need to push on to the great doubt. Need for the Spirit.

Hang on to the clear light!

NOTES

Introduction

1. George Woodcock, *Thomas Merton, Monk and Poet* (New York: Farrar, Straus, Giroux, 1978), p. 11.

2. Br. Patrick Hart to Joel Weishaus, 19 September 1980.

3. James P. Shannon, "Thomas Merton's New Mexico," *New Mexico Magazine* 49, nos. 5-6 (May/June 1971): 18-23.

4. *See* Swami Nityaswarupanada, transl., *Astavakra Samhita* (Hollywood: Vedanta Press, n.d.).

5. John Howard Griffin, *Continuum* 7, no. 2 (Summer 1969): 291.

6. John Howard Griffin, *A Hidden Wholeness: The Visual World of Thomas Merton* (Boston: Houghton Mifflin Co., 1979), p. 50.

7. Ryokan (1758–1831) was a Zen priest, poet and calligrapher. A popular story about Ryokan tells that when his poor hermitage was entered by a would-be thief who could find nothing to carry away, Ryokan, feeling sorry for the man, gave him the clothes he was wearing. After the thief left, Ryokan saw the moon shining through his window and said: "If only I could give him this bright moon!" The translation of Ryokan's poem is by R. H. Blyth in *Haiku,* vol. 1 (Tokyo: The Hokuseido Press, 1949), p. 183.

8. "In Christian terms (suchness) is to see God in an angel as angel, to see God in a flea as flea." D. T. Suzuki, *Zen and Japanese Culture* (New York: Pantheon Books, Inc., 1959), p. 228.

9. Minor White, *Octave of Prayer* (Millerton, N.Y.: Aperture, Inc., 1972), p. 24.

10. Thomas Merton, *The Asian Journal of Thomas Merton* (New York: New Directions Publishing Corp., 1973), p. 153.

11. Emmit Gowin, quoted by Susan Sontag in *On Photography* (New York: Farrar, Straus, Giroux, 1958), p. 200.

12. Thomas Merton, *The Wisdom of the Desert* (New York: New Directions Publishing Corp., 1960).

13. Thomas Merton, *Thoughts in Solitude* (New York: Farrar, Straus, Giroux, 1976), pp. 18, 20.

14. "Enlightenment at death = recognition of one's own formless intellect as 'The Clear Light' & reality itself." Thomas Merton, *Notebook #36: 1968 May-October* (unpublished manuscript). *See also* note to p. 48 in Notes to *Woods, Shore, Desert.*

WOODS, SHORE, DESERT

General Note:

The following include clarifications of references in Merton's text as well as letters written to Joel Weishaus about Merton and the time period covered by the journal. Entries dated after May 20, although seeming at times to have been written on location, were made by Merton after his return to Kentucky.—Editor

Page 3: The *Astavakra Gita,* or *Samhita,* ascribed to a Hindu sage named Astavakra, is a dialogue between him and his disciple, Janaka.

Page 3: Alexander Yelchaninov (1881–1934) was a Russian priest and teacher.

Page 4: Merton's reference to Descartes comes from Georges Poulet, *Studies in Human Time* (Baltimore: The Johns Hopkins Press, 1956), pp. 50–72.

Page 4: For a lengthy exposition of late seventeenth-century Jansenism *see* Dale van Kley, *The Jansenists and the Expulsion of the Jesuits from France* (New Haven and London: Yale University Press, 1975).

Page 4: Charles Augustin Sainte-Beuve (1804–1869) was a French essayist, poet, critic, journalist, professor, senator, and novelist. *See* Sainte-Beuve's *Port Royal* (Paris: Gallimard, 1961). "Voilà presque du scabreux, . . ." translates as "There, nearly scabrous, it seems to me; there the nocturnal falcons of Port Royal."

Page 6: Blaise Pascal (1623–1662) was a child prodigy in mathematics and physics. From 1654 on, residing within the confines of Port Royal, he concentrated on spiritual pursuits. His most famous literary works are the *Pensées* and *Provincial Letters.* All quotes by or with reference to Pascal are from Poulet, *Studies in Human Time,* pp. 74–95.

Page 8: On March 21, 1968, *The New York Times* reported that "about 5,000 sheep have been struck down by some mysterious killing agent . . . suspicion was pointed tonight at nerve gas being tested at the Army's Dugway Proving Ground (Utah)." The Army refused to comment on the incident. Two days later Dr. D. A. Osguthorpe, head of a special investigating team, said, "We are as positive as medical science can ever be" that nerve gas from tests conducted by the Army had killed 6,400 sheep in western Utah's Skull Valley.

Page 9: Alfred Stern, *Sartre. His Philosophy and Existential Psychoanalysis* (New York: Dell Publishing Co., Inc., 1967). Merton quotes the author: "Each philosopher can only give the truth of his existence . . ." Past this quotation, the sentence continues: "Which, however, always offers an essential aspect of human existence as such." (p. 4) In Merton's manuscript perhaps he forgot to insert quotation marks after the word "existence." The balance of the paragraph may either be Merton's words or his quoting from a source I have not been able to locate.

Pages 9-10: The Unamuno quotation is from Stern's *Sartre*, p. 6. Merton inserted the words "whole" and "in" in the last sentence. Stern lists both the Spanish original and the American edition of Miguel de Unamuno's *Del Sentimiento tragico de la Vida* (Madrid, 1913; New York, 1959; American edition, *The Tragic Sense of Life* (New York, Dover Publications, 1954) as his sources.

Page 10: Hegel quote is from Stern's *Sartre,* p. 20. Stern is quoting from *The Logic of Hegel* (Oxford, 1874).

Page 10: Sartre quote is from Stern's *Sartre,* p. 31. The sentence reads: "They tried to overcome their contingency, inventing a necessary Being which is the cause of itself." It is clear from all the quotes from Alfred Stern's book that Merton wasn't concerned with quoting accurately, rather with melding the ideas quoted with his own.

Page 11: "Whitethorn (Our Lady of the Redwoods' location) is located southwest of Garberville (California) where the Mattole River crosses the Mendocino-Humboldt County Line." Sister Veronique Geeroms to Joel Weishaus, 10 October 1980.

Page 14: "Bear Harbor and Needle Rock are both located on the Lost Coast, the black sand beaches along the Pacific west of the monastery." *Ibid.*

Page 17: Wilber H. ("Ping") Ferry is the former Vice-President of The Center for the Study of Democratic Institutions, Santa Barbara, California. He is presently a writer, lecturer and consultant to foundations.

Ferry and his first wife drove Merton from Santa Barbara to Oregon just before Merton left for Asia. Ferry recalls,

We stopped for a couple of days at Redwoods Monastery, south of Eureka and about 20 miles from the coast. The community was relatively new, established by eight or nine Belgian-French Trappist nuns in 1965 or so, as I recall. They fluttered a good deal to have TM in their midst. He bore their attentions with grace. We' drove to the coast which I thought would be utterly deserted. It took us across many miles of logging road, rutted and bunkered with rocks. Tom was entertaining the dream of a hermitage in such a location, and this seemed esp. promising to him because he saw the nuns as his line to the grocery store. But when we, after three hours, finally topped the last demi-mountain & gazed down to the sea, we beheld an almost-completed vacation center, condominiums, playground, and every sign of numerous activities along the strand. So much for that. Our experience was somewhat the same wherever we thrust through to the shore of N. Cal., and also in Oregon.

During these days Tom enjoyed himself. We traveled with a ready stock of Oly(mpia beer). He took pictures & often asked me to stop to gaze on an abandoned barn, a stretch of beach, a sunny valley. He said his office regularly, did not encourage conversation, and clearly had his mind on the Orient much of the time.

But he was coming back, for sure. He raised the question himself . . . and his answer was invariably, 'I'll always be a monk of Gethsemani.' At the same time, he had hoped to have two or three years in (probably) Japan at a Zen Center. And he hoped to find a place to be alone, and away from Gethsemani, to take the solitary road for several years. Whether he intended some time to return physically to G. I don't think he'd decided yet himself. But he certainly wanted to have forever the identification of a monk of Gethsemani.

W. H. Ferry to Joel Weishaus, 20 September 1980.

Page 18: "The Wild Places," *The Center Magazine* (Santa Barbara, California: Fund for the Republic, Inc., July, 1968): 40—44.

Page 20: Thomas Merton, *Journal of My Escape from the Nazis* was published as *My Argument with the Gestapo: A Macaronic Journal* (Garden City: Doubleday & Co., Inc., 1969. Reprint, New York: New Directions Publishing Corp., 1975).

Page 21: Merton received word from New Zealand in April that his Aunt Kit (Merton), aged seventy-nine, had drowned when a ferry boat named the *Wa-*

hine sank. Up until the time her lifeboat capsized she had been seen comforting the other passengers. *See* Monica Furlong, *Merton. A Biography* (San Francisco: Harper & Row, 1980), p. 316.

Page 22: Late T'ang poems can be found in A. C. Graham, transl., *Poems of the Late T'ang* (New York: Penguin Books, 1965).

Page 22: Lawrence Ferlinghetti, poet, publisher of City Lights Books.

Page 22: Sven Heilo "is a Swedish Catholic who corresponded with Merton, has translated Merton into Swedish, and has been active in promoting his writing among Swedish Catholics." Robert E. Daggy to Joel Weishaus, 29 September 1980.

Page 22: *Kora in Hell: Improvisations* (San Francisco: City Lights Paperbook No. 7).

Page 24: "And some, like champions, Fen or Yu . . ." is from "The South Mountains" by Han Yu. *Poems of the Late T'ang,* p. 78.

Page 24: Lu T'ung, *Ibid.,* p. 85.

Pages 26, 28: George Nakashima designed the chapel, which Merton calls "the best monastic building in the country."

Page 28: Fr. Aelred Wall presently lives in San Miguel de Allende, Mexico, where he has "a hermitage and chapel, a wood-working shop, a small farm and a clinic for the benefit of the poor Indians." Fr. Aelred Wall to Joel Weishaus, 15 September 1979.

Page 28: Fr. Gregory Borgstedt "came (to the Monastery of Christ in the Desert) from Mount Saviour in the autumn of 1967— he returned (to Mount Saviour) in March of 1974 with what was eventually diagnosed as cancer, and he died there on December 9th 1975." "One of the Brothers at Monastery of Christ in the Desert" to Joel Weishaus, 21 September 1980.

Page 28: "Quite by accident we ran into one another just before an office in the old chapel, decided to ditch the service and go to my hermitage for what (Fr. Merton) called 'a general chapter of hermits.'

We talked for 2 or 3 hours about the concrete ideal of living as hermits, as well as about the conflicting situations arising between hermits and monastery-dwellers . . . his was a very simple and approachable character, full of humor and sarcasm as to monastic ways." Denis Hines to Joel Weishaus, 21 June 1979.

Page 30: John Howard Griffin is the author of several books, including *A Hidden Wholeness: The Visual World of Thomas Merton* (Boston: Houghton Mifflin Co., 1979). Griffin was chosen by the Trustees of the Merton Legacy Trust to write the authorized biography, but he died before the work was completed. See *The Hermitage Journals* by John Howard Griffin, written while he was researching the biography in Merton's hermitage (Kansas City: Andrews and McMeel, 1981).

Page 30: "Georgia O'Keefe [sic]—a woman of extraordinary quality, live, full of resiliency, awareness, quietness. One of the few people one ever finds (in this country at least) who quietly does everything right. Perfection of her house & patio on ghost ranch, low, hidden in desert rocks & vegetation, but with an extraordinary view of the mountains—especially the great majestic mesa, Pedernal." Thomas Merton, *Notebook #36: 1968 May–October* (unpublished manuscript).

Page 32: Reies Lopez Tijerina is the founder of Alianza, a militant group of Spanish Americans demanding the return of millions of acres of land they contend is their inheritance through old Spanish and Mexican land grants given to their ancestors.

On June 5, 1967, twenty of the militants attacked the Rio Arriba County Courthouse. After a few hours of shouting and shooting, the band fled into the mountains. *See* Peter Nabokov, *Tijerina and the Courthouse Raid* (Albuquerque: University of New Mexico Press, 1969).

Page 32: Peter Nabokov's "book on the Indians" is *Two Leggings: The Making of a Crow Warrior* (New York: Thomas Y. Crowell, 1967).

Page 38: "I'm . . . not sure how conditioned my response to [Merton] was by something I'd read, a snapshot, or a personal description, because I do remember feeling unsurprised by how he was dressed—in Big Mac plumbers clothes or something like that, and how stationed he looked in them, planted like a tree wherever he stood. I felt like a clothes hanger made of wire beside him. His smile was just there, not looking after you or hiding from you." Peter Nabokov to Joel Weishaus, 21 September 1980.

Page 40: All quotes by or with reference to Molière are from Poulet, *Studies in Human Time,* pp. 97–104. As discussed in the note to page 9, Merton's quotes from this book are not accurate.

Page 41: "Qui peut servir de modele" and "chatiment qui peut servir de leçon" translate as "which can serve as a model" and "punishment which can teach a lesson." "La reforme, oui; le chienlit, non!" translates as "Reform, yes; vulgarity, no!"

Page 48: In "Conversation between Professor Maseo Abe and Dom Aelred Graham in Kyoto, August 26, 1967," Professor Abe says: "First of all you should meet Dr. (Shinichi) Hisamatsu, my teacher. He is a genuine Zen man. He is not a priest, but a layman. But in my view he is a much more profound and genuine Zen man than any master, and he has a very deep Zen realization, as well as a philosophical mind." *Conversations: Christian and Buddhist, Dom Aelred Graham* (New York: Harcourt Brace Jovanovich, Inc., 1968), p. 15.

Page 48: Merton's thoughts on not having to "work on myself," and "right effort," are in the spirit of Zen teaching: there is nothing to achieve, as we are already enlightened, or in-Christ; only our self-centered conditioned thinking stands in the way of realization. The harder we work, which is merely our egos defining themselves, the further we move away from Original Mind.

Page 48: On Clear Light, Mircea Eliade wrote:

> Death is a process of cosmic reabsorption, not in the sense that the flesh returns to the earth, but in the sense that the cosmic elements progressively dissolve into one another . . .
>
> When the process of cosmic reabsorption is complete, the dying man perceives a light like that of the Moon, then like that of the Sun, then sinks deep into the darkness. He is suddenly awakened by a dazzling light: this is his meeting with his real Self, which, according to the doctrine of all India, is at the same time the ultimate reality, Being.

Mircea Eliade, "Light and the Bardo," *The Two and the One* (New York: Harper & Row, 1965), pp. 37–38.